...CHER COLLECTION

SING A SONG OF SCIENCE

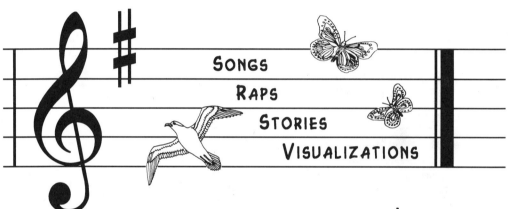

SONGS

RAPS

STORIES

VISUALIZATIONS

KATHLEEN CARROLL

Zephyr Press ®

REACHING THEIR HIGHEST POTENTIAL
TUCSON, ARIZONA

Sing a Song of Science

Grades: 2–6

© 1999 by Zephyr Press
Printed in the United States of America

ISBN 1-56976-090-X

Editors: Veronica Durie and Stacey Shropshire
Cover Design: Daniel Miedaner
Illustrations: Steve Carroll
Design and Production: Daniel Miedaner

Zephyr Press
PO Box 66006
Tucson, AZ 85738-6006
1-800-232-2187
http\\:www.zephyrpress.com

Library of Congress Cataloging-in-Publication Data

Carroll, Kathleen, 1946-
    Sing a song of science / Kathleen Carroll.
      p.   cm.
    Includes bibliographical references.
    ISBN 1-56976-090-X (alk. paper)
    1. Science—Study and teaching (Elementary)—Activity programs.
  2. Children's songs. I. Title.
LB1585.C295 1999
372.3'5—dc21   98-36097

CONTENTS

INTRODUCTION
Ⓢ BRAIN-FRIENDLY TEACHING

This book was created out of necessity. Some years ago, my school district introduced districtwide science tests at the elementary and middle school levels. I was the science resource teacher for my school at the time. I found that, while my students were benefiting in many ways from the hands-on experiences in science class, the results of their learning were not being reflected on written tests. I felt forced to stretch into new approaches to teaching so that students would learn with joy, engagement, and creativity, *and* do well on standardized tests.

Sometimes a hands-on approach used alone can leave students without the words to express the concepts they have begun to understand. To do well on tests, students need to acquire the vocabulary and context to express concepts they learn through their investigations. Students also need to understand where the new concepts fit in the larger scheme of things.

The book and audiotape set *Sing a Song of Science* grew out of an attempt to solve this problem. Through my exposure to the research summarized in the following sections, I came to understand the need for story, along with hands-on investigations, in teaching science. *Sing a Song of Science* demonstrates the use of song, rap, and narrative that teachers can use after students have had concrete experiences with scientific phenomena and reflected on the experiences themselves.

Researchers have been making huge strides in our understanding of how people learn. *Sing a Song of Science* illustrates some practical, student-tested ways to use the results of educational research in the classroom.

ACCELERATED LEARNING

Accelerated learning methodologies are the result of more than thirty years of research by Georgi Lozanov (1981), a Bulgarian psychologist. Lozanov's goal was to discover how people could use their brains more effectively in learning. Over time, he designed a system that aptly employed stories, music, games, laughter, and fun during learning situations. Lozanov found that his approach broke down people's barriers to learning, making it possible for them to take in enormous amounts of information very rapidly. Many innovators have built their research on Lozanov's breakthrough discoveries (Brewer and Campbell 1991; Dryden and Vos 1995).

ENRICHED ENVIRONMENTS

Marian Diamond (1985) has done extensive research on the positive effects of enriched environments. In *A Celebration of Neurons*, Robert Sylwester (1995) reflects on some implications of Diamond's research for the classroom:

- Adding music, stories, and role-play to more traditional techniques can enrich the environment in a classroom.
- Using multiple entry points to introduce a concept can actually increase the neurological connections, thus the learning of the concept.
- It is not enough to expose students to a stimulating environment dominated by a teacher. Students must have opportunities to personally interact with and help create the enriched environment to fully experience its positive effects.

MULTIPLE INTELLIGENCE THEORY

Almost fifteen years ago, Howard Gardner of Harvard University used brain biology and other evidence to take a fresh look at the nature of intelligence. In *Frames of Mind* (1985), the original book that presented his findings, Gardner describes five intelligences that can be isolated in the brain in addition to the verbal-linguistic and logical-mathematical intelligences that IQ tests measure. These intelligences include visual-spatial, musical-rhythmic, bodily-kinesthetic, interpersonal (self with others), and intrapersonal (self with self). In 1995, Gardner and his associates identified an eighth intelligence, the naturalist. In an interview with *Educational Leadership* (Checkley 1997), Gardner describes the naturalist intelligence as the ability to recognize and classify animals and plants as well as nonliving things, such as clouds, rocks, and minerals. Many teachers agree with Gardner that in the real world these other intelligences are equal in value to the verbal-linguistic and logical-mathematical intelligences that traditional education has emphasized. All the intelligences deserve to be developed in their own right and a variety of intelligences can be used in lessons to enhance students' learning of any subject matter. Teaching to all eight intelligences gives all types of learners an opportunity to lead with their strengths, at least part of the time, as they learn to develop their weaker intelligences.

Following are some specific instructional methods used in *Sing a Song of Science*.

Stories

Introducing science units with stories that include relevant concepts and vocabulary is a powerful way for students to take in information. Stories involve the emotions and emotions are essential ingredients for long-term memory. Stories also enhance memory by logically sequencing facts so that each subsequent piece of information is placed within the context of the previous information. Presenting facts in context enhances recall (Jensen 1995; Sylwester 1995).

Storytelling also makes teaching easier. The students are quiet and listen well with this method since it is human nature to want to hear a good story. Storytelling is far more brain friendly than lectures. Making up stories also helps teachers breathe new life into the subject matter they teach and discover new levels of creativity in themselves.

One approach that I took in my own teaching, particularly with older elementary and middle school students, was to present stories about real people that relate to the subject matter. For instance, when I introduced the subject of weather to fifth graders, I told them about Floyd Abell, who lives in Hollywood, Maryland, and is a volunteer weather watcher for the local TV weather reporter, Bob Ryan. As I informed students about Floyd Abell's hobby, the instruments he uses and how much he loves keeping track of the weather, some of my students started thinking, "Maybe I want to do this, too." The story would spark the students' attention and, since attention drives learning, they began to master the instructional objectives just from hearing the story. I also recounted the trials of Thomas Edison, Louis Pasteur, and Elizabeth Blackwell. Teaching through biography brings science to life.

I sometimes used storytelling, particularly with younger students, to create fantasy to teach fact. I made up a story that creates a memorable context for the essential learning about the subject. For instance, when teaching about humanmade and natural objects, I often told a story of a boy and girl who travel in a time machine to a time before there were any humans. Students pictured what their neighborhood might have looked like in its natural state and the ways in which humans have changed it over time. Students also learned about the principles involved in expansion and contraction through one of my stories. A boy in the city loses his helium-filled balloon and a girl in the country finds it when the weather becomes cooler and the helium contracts. Zorky, the Zircon, a child from another galaxy who visits our solar system, introduced my students to astronomy. At the end of the story, the class made lists that clarify which aspects of the story relate facts and which aspects are fiction.

VISUALIZATION

Visualization is the brain's ability to create internal pictures. The development of high levels of imagination and problem-solving ability is linked to the capacity to visualize. The constant overstimulation children receive from television hinders them in making their own internal pictures and impedes the development of this important ability (Hannaford 1995).

Purposefully using visualization in the classroom can help to counteract some of the damage television has done. Visualization creates more brain connections for learning. The connections are formed by some brain functions that have traditionally been ignored or frowned upon in school. These functions include daydreaming, fantasizing, creating images, doodling, and nonlinear, nonverbal, timeless, holistic ways of perceiving the world. Allowed their place in learning, these functions can be important components of creativity.

In the sense the term is used here, visualization is similar to story telling, except that the story is told in a way that leads students to see, feel, hear, smell, and taste as if they were actually experiencing the events described. When you present a visualization to a group, the participants get into a relaxed state; then you guide them on an inner journey. Students can experience the "Big Bang" theory of the beginning of the universe and watch galaxies, solar systems, and our Earth as they form. At other times students can ride a light beam with Einstein as he discovers the principles of relativity. They can become a molecule of oxygen as it travels through the blood stream or visit the land of metric and meet the metric units of measurement. Music can be an exciting addition to visualization, but it is not necessary. Visualization exercises the visual-spatial and intrapersonal intelligences.

SONGS AND RAPS

Rhythm, rhyme, and music, as they tap into the musical intelligence, are brain-friendly ways of getting across information. Robert Sylwester (1995) notes "songs go far beyond words in their ability to insert emotion into communication" (109). Since emotion is a cornerstone of memory, the musical intelligence can be a tremendous resource for learning any subject matter. We all know how much easier it is for students to remember lyrics of songs and raps from the current pop station than it is for them to remember science concepts. We adults often use similar aids, such as "Thirty days hath September, April, June, and November . . . " to help us remember information.

My students needed to improve their ability to talk about science concepts and to demonstrate their learning on tests, so I began to experiment with creating songs and raps that would reinforce the vocabulary and the essential ideas. The first time I presented a rap, I noticed a number of students scrambling to copy it. I was amazed when I took them on field trip a few days later to find that most of the students spent the bus ride reciting the rap in unison. Realizing that I was on to something, I began to introduce songs and raps in all my classes. From then on, students often walked into my classroom singing the song that related to the current science objective.

Using raps for teaching is a way to bring right into the classroom a mode of communication young people have developed themselves. Students are enthusiastic because they find it possible to integrate school with the rest of their lives, which gives them a chance to be actively involved instead of just "talked at."

Raps that present new ideas and vocabulary are easy to design. Students will also find it fun and motivating to write raps, which can enable them to synthesize the information they have been studying and to present it to the rest of the class. Creating raps related to the subject matter enhances self-esteem, especially the self-esteem of students who have not been very successful academically.

Sherwin and Nathaniel are two prime examples. They tended to be truant a lot and were streetwise; neither was interested in academics. One day I suggested that the class choose a body system and make up raps about it. I had never seen Sherwin and Nathaniel so excited. They stayed after school to work on their rap and even created a carefully drawn, full-color poster of the digestive system for the performance. The other students were an appreciative audience. The only problem with this method is toning down the enthusiasm—a problem I don't mind having!

MIND MAPPING

The Mind Mapping method of taking notes was developed by Tony Buzan of Oxford. This method combines the creativity of the right brain and the logic and orderliness of the left brain. With Mind Mapping, a synergy that greatly enhances learning and recall takes place. The technique also develops the visual-spatial and interpersonal intelligences when students work with others and the intrapersonal intelligence when students work alone.

To make a Mind Map, write or draw the main idea in the center. Branch out with words and pictures, one to a line. Arrows show connections between ideas. Asterisks, exclamation points, and big writing show emphasis. The branches can be drawn or written in various colors so the eye can easily distinguish among the branches.

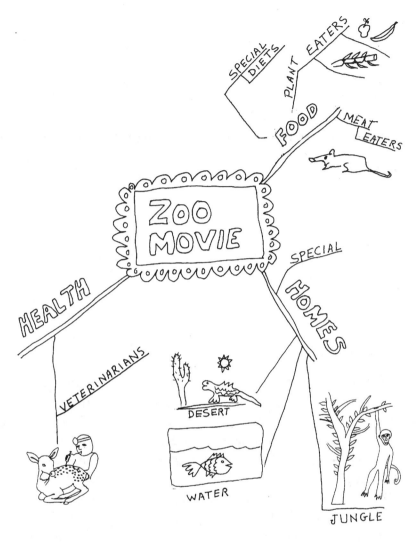

Use Mind Mapping to introduce new units of study. Ask students to Mind Map what they know about the subject so they get to do most of the talking; you'll discover and clear up any misconceptions they may have along the way.

Students love working in groups to make large Mind Maps of what will be covered during the semester or to show what they have learned. They also enjoy Mind Mapping their ideas before creative writing sessions.

Following is a practical example of a way Mind Mapping has worked in my teaching: An official from the National Zoo wanted to field test a film to find out if it was appropriate for first grade. She showed the film in two schools. One was an upper-middle-class school in one of the most affluent neighborhoods of Washington, D.C. The other was my school in the heart of the inner city, where practically all the students would be considered "disadvantaged." The zoo official presented me with a list of convergent questions such as "What is the name of the doctor who takes care of sick animals?" Instead of using them I asked divergent questions that drew information from the students organically, in a nonthreatening way. I just started with "What did you learn from this film?" As each child responded, I mapped key words and pictures on the chalkboard with colored chalks. These key words and pictures acted as hooks for other students' thinking. By the time we completed the discussion, these little children had given an extremely detailed report of every aspect of the film.

As I walked the zoo official to the door, she looked very confused. "Sometimes our preconceptions turn out to be misconceptions," she said. "I thought the children from the middle-class school would get more from the film. It turns out, though, that your children learned far more then they did." In truth, the children at my school probably had not learned any more from the film than the other students. The difference was that the information had been drawn from them in a way more compatible with how the brain works.

KINESTHETIC LEARNING

With kinesthetic learning, students act out the concepts they are learning through games or role-play. Barbara Clark (1986) of California State University called this method "physical encoding." Physical movement is far more important to learning than was previously thought (Sylwester 1995). The more neurological connections a person makes in response to a particular piece of learning, the greater the retention. Kinesthetic methods help to encode learning in more parts of the brain than do traditional learning approaches. Kinesthetic learning can help develop the intelligence Howard Gardner refers to as the bodily-kinesthetic intelligence. For some learners who learn primarily through physical movement, adding kinesthetic activities means the difference between success and failure in school.

Kinesthetic methods lend themselves to a wide variety of uses in the classroom. My students acted out the workings of the digestive system—one student became the hamburger while others became various organs that acted on the hamburger. The students' role-played the various body systems, which also served as an alternative assessment of their understanding of the structure and functions of the system and of their ability to cooperate in solving a problem. Sometimes students formed groups to act out the food chain—one student was the sun, another a plant, another an animal who eats the plant. The plant eater was attacked by a meat-eating animal who eventually died and gave her energy to the plant. Sixth graders also made up skits to show the best way to deal with situations that involved drugs, including cigarettes and alcohol. After kindergartners worked with magnets, they became magnets, attracting and repelling each other. Third graders became molecules of water, clustering together as solids, then spreading apart as liquids and gases. For bilateral symmetry, I turned on music and students matched each others' movements as they chanted "bilateral symmetry."

It's easy to remember how a system works when you are a part of that system. Students were especially enthusiastic when we made videos of their original plays. Little did they know that watching the video was serving as another opportunity to review the concepts they were learning.

THE RESULTS

Since I started teaching with these techniques, even the driest subject matter has become enjoyable. Test scores have improved. Students who disliked science in the past have become enthusiastic participants. Hands-on activities are the most important components in a science program. The techniques described in the previous sections expand and reinforce students' learning.

Many teachers in the workshops and courses I teach have been surprised at how easy it is to let their creativity flow into making science fun and memorable. Teachers have also been excited about their students' abilities to use their own creativity to enhance their learning.

The generation that is growing up today will be faced with some of the most important decisions in our Earth's history. If we as a species are to survive and thrive in the twenty-first century, we need a scientifically literate population. We also need people who are capable of focusing their unbounded creativity and inventiveness into solving the problems at hand. We need to make science appealing to all students. Brain-friendly strategies bring a quality of lightness, fun, and creativity to a nonthreatening atmosphere; they make learning easy. These strategies can be used in any classroom.

THE QUESTION OF ANTHROPOMORPHISM

Anthropomorphism attributes human qualities to animals, plants, or nonliving things. Examples of anthropomorphism are in fairy tales, where the wolf speaks to Little Red Riding Hood, and in fables, where Br'er Turtle and Br'er Rabbit compete in a race. Anthropomorphism can also be found in animated films such as *Beauty and the Beast*, where teacups and teakettles dance and sing. Children are constantly surrounded by anthropomorphism, from Barney, Miss Piggy, and Teenage Mutant Ninja Turtles to socializing M & Ms and Sonic, the Hedgehog.

Most children realize that real teacups and M & Ms are not able to dance and sing. They can discern the difference between make-believe and real life in regard to plants and inanimate objects. They may, however, be less discriminating in regard to animals. We can help them make the distinction, providing a valuable learning experience while we do so.

Some scientists, in their effort to avoid anthropomorphism, may go too far, as in denying emotions exist in animals. Many pet owners can share stories that indicate their pets' expression of emotions.

You can use the stories and songs in *Sing a Song of Science* to help students clarify their thinking. Simply introduce the stories and songs with "Let's pretend." Follow up by making an experience chart on which students list the make-believe and the real messages from the stories and songs. Students can also work alone or in cooperative learning groups to develop lists.

How to Use the Book and Tape

The stories and visualizations can serve as an overview to introduce a science unit. Some of the longer songs and raps such as the "Human Body Song," the "Energy Rap," and "Tropical Rain Forest Rap" can be used as an overview, as well. Giving a broad overview before introducing specific facts is a special help to those students who are field dependent. These students, and there are many of them, learn best when they get the whole picture before they learn specific facts.

The students can sing the songs or say the raps every day that you are studying the unit, which will help them have fun remembering the vocabulary and concepts. Individual groups of students can Mind Map a song or story to give them a visual hook into the information. After the visualizations, students can write about their experiences to translate their visual images to language. Describing a mental image in words increases the connections between the brain hemispheres and, according to some studies, measurably increases intelligence (Wenger and Poe 1996).

Within the book are specific suggestions for hands-on activities, additional ways to use the songs, raps, and stories, and web connections to reinforce the content. Some addresses you might like to visit with your students appear at the end of the lessons.

I hope these songs, stories, activities, and other techniques serve as models for you to create your own or have students create for you. The activities offer opportunities to develop higher-level thinking skills such as analysis and synthesis. They also offer a way to make teaching and learning more fun and memorable for everyone. Enjoy!

MATTER SONG

I'M A MOLECULE OF WATER,
AND BY MYSELF I'M SORTER
A LITTLE TOO SMALL TO SEE.
BUT WHEN I FREEZE TOGETHER TIGHTLY
WITH A ZILLION OTHERS LIKE ME,
WE MAKE SOLID COMPANY. THAT'S ICE!

REFRAIN:

O MATTER. WHAT DOES IT MATTER?
WELL, LET'S JUST MAKE A CASE:
THERE'S MATTER IN THE WATER
AND A TREE AND AIR AND DAUGHTER.
MATTER IS EV'RY PLACE.

WHEN I'M SITTING BY THE FIRE,
AND GETTING TO PERSPIRE
IT'S THEN I START TO FLOW.
I MELT INTO A PUDDLE
AND IT ISN'T VERY SUBTLE,
I'M A LIQUID THEN YOU KNOW. THAT'S WATER!

[REFRAIN]

AND IF THAT FIRE KEEPS BURNING,
I MAY JUST GET A YEARNING
FOR A DIFFERENT SORT OF FATE.
AND I'LL RACE AROUND SO FREELY
THAT IT'S VERY HARD TO SEE ME.
THAT'S HOW I EVAPORATE. WHAT A GAS!

[REFRAIN]

SOLID, LIQUID, AND GAS!!

1

Matter Song

Words and Music by
Kathleen Carroll

1. I'm a mo-le-cule of wa-ter, and
2. When I'm sit-ting by the fire, and
3. And if that fire keeps burn-ing, I

by my-self I'm sor-ter a lit-tle too small to see.____ But when I
get-ting to per-spi-re, it's then I start to flow.____ I
may just get a yearn-ing for a dif-fer-ent sort of fate.____ And I'll

freeze to-geth-er tight-ly with a zil-lion oth-ers like me,____
melt in-to a pud-dle and it is-n't ver-y sub-tle,____
race a-round so free-ly that it's ve-ry hard to see me.____

we make so-lid com-pa-ny. **(spoken)** *That's ice!*
I'm a li-quid then you know. *That's water!*
That's how I e-vap-o-rate. *What a gas!*

O mat-ter, what does it mat-ter? Well, let's just make a case:

There's mat-ter in the wa-ter and a tree and air and daugh-ter.____

Mat-ter is ev'-ry place.____ (place) sol-id li-quid and gas!

Some Ideas for Learning about Matter

⧉ Students mark the level of water in a cup, then check it again after a few days. They speculate about why the water level is lower and compare their ideas with those of other students. They devise experiments to test their hypotheses, which can lead them to discover the principle of evaporation.

⧉ Give individual students a piece of ice in a cup. They experiment with ways to make the ice melt faster, for example, by rubbing the ice quickly between their hands. They discuss their findings with one another and look for common results. They will discover that it takes heat to melt a solid to a liquid. Discuss other examples of solids that melt with heat (butter melts in the frying pan, soap melts in a hot shower, metal melts in a smelter).

⧉ Students put the water from the melted ice into a pan on a hot plate, then predict the results of heating the water, which will give students another experience of evaporation.

⧉ Give individual students a plastic cup that contains ice and colored water. Students observe the outside of the cups carefully as condensation begins to form. Students make inferences about the source of the condensation. Students often infer that the water on the outside of the cup has seeped through tiny holes in the cup. Make sure they notice that the liquid on the inside of the cup is a different color from that on the outside of the cup. The source of condensation, whether on a glass filled with ice, a windowpane, or a mirror in a bathroom, is invisible water vapor in the air that condenses into liquid. Cold temperatures condense a gas to liquid and colder temperatures freeze liquids to solids.

Some Ways to Use the Song

⧉ Groups of students act out "Matter Song." Each member of the group represents a molecule. Members of each group role-play a solid by coming close together and vibrating slightly. They move further apart to represent a liquid. They role-play evaporation when they race around so freely.

⧉ Students listen to the "Water Cycle" visualization, then write and illustrate their own stories about the water cycle. Encourage them to use vocabulary that relates to changing states of matter.

⧉ Groups of students list elements of the "Matter Song" and the "Water Cycle" visualization into two categories, real and make-believe. Groups compare their lists and discuss discrepancies.

WEB ADDRESSES

http://www.halcyon.com/marcs/science.html

This site has an exciting inquiry lesson on matter. Students use their knowledge of the states of matter to solve a mystery from the story, "Encyclopedia Brown and the Case of the Secret Pitch."

http://www.iit.edu/~smile/ph9316.html

Look here for a lesson on the states of matter that includes making No Bake Cookies.

LAYERS OF THE EARTH SONG

REFRAIN:
THE CRUST, THE MANTLE, THE CORE (CLICK, CLICK)*
THE CRUST, THE MANTLE, THE CORE (CLICK, CLICK)
THESE ARE THREE PARTS OF THE PLANET EARTH,
NOW LET ME TELL YOU MORE. (CLICK, CLICK)

SOIL AND WATER MAKE THE CRUST,
NOW THAT'S THE PART YOU KNOW.
AND IN THE CRUST THERE'S BEDROCK, TOO,
BUT THAT PART DOESN'T SHOW.

[REFRAIN]

THE MANTLE IS HOT, SQUISHY ROCK
ON WHICH THE CRUST CAN SLIDE.
AND THAT IS WHY OUR CONTINENTS
ARE GOING FOR A RIDE.

[REFRAIN]

IRON AND NICKEL MAKE THE CORE
THAT'S MELTED THROUGH AND THROUGH.
NOW NO ONE'S EVER SEEN THE CORE;
IT'S WHAT WE THINK IS TRUE.

FINAL REFRAIN:

THE CRUST, THE MANTLE, THE CORE (CLICK, CLICK)
THE CRUST, THE MANTLE, THE CORE (CLICK, CLICK)
THESE ARE THREE PARTS OF PLANET EARTH
THAT'S ALL WE HAD IN STORE! (CLICK, CLICK)

*SNAP TONGUE AGAINST ROOF OF MOUTH.

Layers of the Earth Song

Words and Music by
Kathleen Carroll

SOME IDEAS FOR LEARNING ABOUT THE EARTH LAYERS

■ Students use red, yellow, blue, and green clay or Play Dough to make a model of Earth's layers. For instance, students might make a small red ball as they discuss the properties of Earth's core. They cover the red ball with yellow as they discuss the mantle. They make the green continents and blue oceans as they discuss the crust. A cut through the model with a pin or plastic knife makes all the layers visible.

■ The song mentions that the crust "can slide" and that the "continents are going for a ride." These lines provide a lead-in to the study of plate tectonics and to studies of earthquakes and volcanoes. Refer to the web sites for some exciting ways to learn about how movements deep within Earth are changing its shape every day.

SOME WAYS TO USE THE SONG

■ Use "Layers of the Earth Song" as an interactive bulletin board. Students make a large colorful drawing of Earth's layers, or you could use a commercial picture of Earth's layers. Type lines from each stanza of the song on cards and place them below the picture with a string and pin attached. Instructions on the bulletin board ask students to place the pin connected to each description into the appropriate element of the picture.

WEB ADDRESSES

http://www.jasonproject.org/
JASON/HTML/EXPEDITIONS_JASON_8_home.html

The Jason Project, a project that involves students all over the United States in original research with scientists, has a site based on Jason VIII, Journey from the Center of the Earth. The curriculum is based on the study of two geologically active sites, Iceland and Yellowstone.

http://www.earthweek.com/

This site presents Earthweek, a Diary of the Planet, from Discovery On-line News. Earthweek presents a map of the world with symbols that highlight the natural and humanmade events of the week that affect Earth's environment. Links to other sites provide background knowledge about the week's events.

http://www.usgs.gov/education/index.html

This site from the US Geological Survey's Learning Web provides lessons and background information on many topics that involve the study of earth science. Topics include the study of volcanoes and earthquakes, the use of satellites to study Earth, and more. Students can e-mail earth science questions to: Ask -A-Geologist@usgs.gov

ENERGY RAP

WIND CAN, WIND CAN, WIND CAN BE
A TERRIFIC SOURCE OF ENERGY.
IT'S VERY, VERY CHEAP, YOU KNOW,
BUT THEN SOMETIMES IT DOES NOT BLOW!

REFRAIN:
WE NEED A SOURCE OF ENERGY
FOR HEAT, TRANSPORTATION, ELECTRICITY!

WATER, WATER, WATER CAN BE
A TERRIFIC SOURCE OF ENERGY.
IT TURNS THINGS HERE, IT TURNS THINGS THERE,
BUT YOU CAN'T FIND WATER EVERYWHERE.

[REFRAIN]

OIL, OIL, OIL CAN BE
A TERRIFIC SOURCE OF ENERGY.
IT'S EASY AS CAN BE TO STORE,
BUT WHEN IT RUNS OUT WE WON'T HAVE MORE.

[REFRAIN]

COAL, COAL, COAL CAN BE
A TERRIFIC SOURCE OF ENERGY.
IT'S EASY AS CAN BE TO STORE,
BUT IT POLLUTES OUR AIR, FOR SURE!

[REFRAIN]

SUN CAN, SUN CAN, SUN CAN BE
A TERRIFIC SOURCE OF ENERGY.
IT'S CHEAP, IT'S CLEAN, IT'S REALLY FINE,
BUT HALF THE DAY IT DOES NOT SHINE!

EASY TO STORE, CLEAN, AND FREE,
A TERRIFIC SOURCE OF ENERGY.
WHEN YOU GROW UP MAYBE YOU'LL FIND
THE PERFECT SOURCE FOR HUMANKIND.

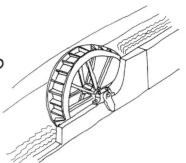

SOME IDEAS FOR LEARNING ABOUT ENERGY SOURCES

⊠ Students check with their parents about methods used to heat their homes. The class makes a graph that shows the distribution of energy sources used. Placed the graph above a resource table that provides information about energy sources and samples of energy sources, such as a can of motor oil and a piece of coal.

⊠ Students research the energy sources used to make electricity in their communities.

⊠ Students ask their parents to show them the electric meter for their homes. They keep track of the amount of electricity used over the course of a few days. When an appliance that consumes a lot of electricity, such as an iron, is on, they observe the electric meter. They may be surprised to see how fast the dial on that meter moves!

⊠ Students use cardboard or tag board to construct a model of a water wheel (see cutout 1). They cut along the solid line, then fold each cut along the dotted line in the same direction. By placing a straight pin or nail in the center of the wheel and setting the wheel under a stream of water, students observe how water turns the wheel. They find ways water turning wheels produces electricity at hydroelectric plants. They also study the impacts that diverting water to make electricity has had on the environments where these plants have been built.

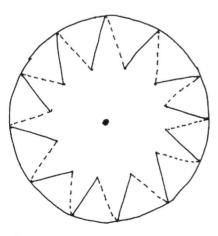

CUTOUT 1

SOME WAYS TO USE THE RAP

⊠ Students choreograph their own dance to go with the "Energy Rap."

⊠ Place students in groups and assign each group an energy source. The group makes a poster using the information in the song along with other references on the advantages and disadvantages of that energy source. As the rap is played, each group's members raise their poster during the stanza that describes their assigned energy source.

WEB ADDRESSES

http://www.eren.doe.gov/

EREN stands for the Energy Efficiency and Renewable Energy Network from the US Department of Energy. This site provides fact sheets about renewable sources of energy; organizations to write to for books on science lessons on energy; kids stuff; science lessons on solar, wind, and other renewable energy sources; and "Ask an Energy Expert." There are also links to many other energy education sites.

http://www.energy.ca.gov/education/

This graphically pleasing website is called Energy Quest and is maintained by California's Energy Commission. Depending on where you click on the picture, you can find a history of fossil fuels written for kids, science projects, stories, energy safety tips, ideas for saving energy, art contests, stories, puzzles, and a lot more.

http://nyelabs.kcts.org/nyeverse/episode/e45.html

Bill Nye the Science Guy's web site has surprising facts and hands-on activities students can do themselves. The activities are based on episodes of his popular TV show, which is sponsored by the National Science Foundation. There are also web links to other interesting science education sites. Bill's presentation on energy at this site gives students a good background on the nature of energy and a fun activity that uses energy to launch a model rocket.

http://www.solarenergy.org/

This home page for Solar Energy International (SEI) lists workshops for learning about renewable energy sources and provides links to government agencies, nonprofit organizations and publications about energy.

http://www.accessone.com/~sbcn/index.htm

This site describes some real-life, solar-energy success stories.

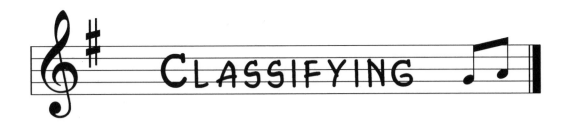

CLASSIFYING

REFRAIN:

CLASSIFYING, CLASSIFYING.
HOW DO YOU DO IT?
PUT THE ONES THAT MATCH TOGETHER.
THERE'S NOTHING TO IT.

A TRIANGLE HAS 3 SIDES, YOU KNOW,
AND A CIRCLE IS ROUND.
WHEN I PUT MY SHAPES
JUST WHERE THEY GO,
I MAKE A HAPPY SOUND. HA, HA, HA!

[REFRAIN]

ALL MY SOCKS GO IN ONE DRAW'R.
MY PANTS GO IN ANOTHER.
WHEN I CLASSIFY MY STUFF
IT REALLY HELPS MY MOTHER.

[REFRAIN]

WE CLASSIFY THINGS EV'RY DAY,
SPOONS AND BIRDS AND BOOKS.
IN OUR WORK AND IN OUR PLAY,
ITS EV'RYWHERE WE LOOK. HA, HA, HA!

[REFRAIN]

11

Classifying

Words and Music by
Kathleen Carroll

Refrain

Class - i - fy - ing, class - i - fy - ing. How do you do it?

Put the ones that match to - geth - er. There's no - thing to it.

1. A tri - an - gle has 3 sides, you know, and a
2. All my socks go in one draw'r My
3. We class - i - fy things ev - 'ry day,

cir - cle is round. When I put my shapes just where they go, I
pants go in an - oth - er. When I class - i - fy my stuff it
spoons and birds and books. In our work and in our play, it's

1, 3.
make a hap - py sound, Ha, Ha, Ha!
ev - 'ry - where we look. Ha, Ha, Ha!

2.
real - ly helps my moth - er.

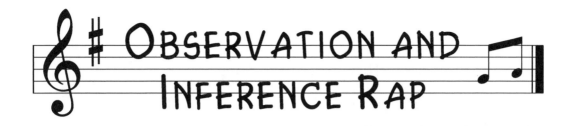

Observation and Inference Rap

An observation is what you know
because your senses tell you so.
"I see . . . ," "I feel . . . ," "I smell . . . ," "I hear . . . ,"
Words make observations clear.

An inference is a good guess;
It's nothing more and nothing less.
"I think . . . ," "It might . . . ," and "probably . . . ,"
Shows it's an inference, you see.

Remember what I'm telling you.
An observation you know is true.
An inference you can't be sure.
It's a good guess, nothing more.

Ideas for Learning about Classification, Observation, and Inference

To classify, students need materials. Since almost any group of objects will do, students can easily gather materials to classify. Take students on a walk outside to collect objects such as leaves, acorns, rocks. Ask students to bring in ten to twenty objects from home. Give each student some of the contents from a bag of fifteen-bean soup. Classifying the beans could be tied in with the plant activities suggested below.

- Ask students to use their senses to observe and describe the objects. Students make inferences or guesses about who brought certain objects into the classroom, how the objects were made, or what would happen if the objects were dropped, put in water, or changed in some way.

- Students classify the objects according to criteria they develop. Young children may not have the maturity to classify. They may use the objects to make pictures of faces, houses, and other objects instead.

- If students have the maturity to consider actual properties of objects (size, shape, color, texture, and so on), ask them to put all the objects into two or three groups. Note that recognizing properties depends on observation skills. Practice classifying improves observation skills as well as classifying skills.

- Without being told the property a student used to classify a group of objects, have other students make inferences about the property used. Other students add a few new objects to the classifying student's groups, which will give the student who made the original groups immediate feedback about how clear the classification system was. Students discuss the properties used to sort the objects.

Some Ways to Use the Song and Rap

- Students often like to sing "Classifying" as they gather materials to design classification systems. Invite them to add stanzas that describe objects to classify that aren't mentioned in the song.

⬚ Use "Classifying" as a game. Groups of four students compete in a round table. The object of the game is to list more classification systems found in school and at home than the other groups list. The four students pass around a piece of paper and a pencil as quickly as possible, with each student adding to the list of classification systems. Examples from the song include books, silverware, and clothes. Other home examples are CDs, audiotapes, and videotapes; food in the refrigerator and food in cabinets; cleaning supplies; spices; *TV Guide;* and the sections of the newspaper. School classification systems students might mention include library materials, math manipulatives, art supplies, student portfolios, the teacher's records of student grades and attendance, and on and on. It helps students to realize that classification pervades their lives.

⬚ Use "Observation and Inference Rap" as the basis for a game. One student secretly places an object in a bag and another student puts one hand into the bag without looking. Before doing so, though, all players will chant the rap, which reinforces the guesser's use of words that describe observations—*feel, smell, hear*—and words that connote inferences—*think, might, probably.*

WEB ADDRESSES

www. monarchwatch.com.

> This site presents real-world opportunities for students to use their science process skills. Students collect data on the life cycles and migrations of monarch butterflies.

http://sln.fi.edu/tfi/units/life/

> At this site, the Franklin Institute Science Museum provides an online curriculum for living things curriculum, which presents classification of plants and animals, including Granddad's Animal Alphabet Books for grades K through 3 and 4 through 6.

http://oaktree.dpi.state.nc.us/Curriculum/Science/process.htm

http://www.enc.org/reform/fworks/ENC2863/28639.htm

> The sites for the science curriculum for the states of North Carolina and Iowa, respectively. Both are based on science process skills. They present hierarchies for teaching process skills.

http://science.coe.uwf.edu/NARST/research/skill.htm

> This site presents research on the effectiveness of directly teaching process skills to help students develop thinking abilities.

How the Girl Learned Pitch

THE SKY IS HIGH
THE SKY IS HIGH

Once there was a little girl who lived in a cottage in a meadow by the woods. One sunny day, she was lying in the grass feeling pretty bored, when suddenly some sparkling lights appeared and darted into the woods.

"Oh! How beautiful!" the little girl exclaimed. "I must follow them and see where they are going." So she scrambled up and ran after them just in time to see that the lights were actually little fairies. They disappeared down a hole in the trunk of the tree right near the edge of the woods.

The little girl arrived at the trunk of the tree just in time to see a frog in a blue jacket shutting a wooden door over the hole in the tree.

"Oh, please let me in!" begged the little girl.

"You have to know the secret passwords," croaked the frog.

But the little girl didn't know the secret passwords. So she sat down and cried. She cried so hard that her tears fell on the ground. The ground took pity on her and said, "Don't cry. I can help you with this poem:

"The roots are low, the roots are low," he said in a low voice.

"That is the sound that you must know."

"Oh, thank you," she said, and ran to the little door.

"The roots are low, the roots are low," she said in a flat tone.

"That is the sound that you must know."

"Not good enough," croaked the frog.

"Why not?" cried the girl, and back came the tears.

Her crying was so loud that she woke up the sky. It said, "It's no problem, little girl. You need the other part of the password, and it's this:

"The sky is high, the sky is high," it said in a high pitch.

"That is the sound that you must cry."

"Oh, thank you. Thank you!" she said. "Now, I've got it straight."

She ran up to the little door and said:

"The roots are low, the roots are low," in a flat tone.

"That is the sound that you must know.

"The sky is high, the sky is high," she said in a flat tone.

"That is the sound that you must cry."

"Not good enough," croaked the frog.

What was missing? That's right, it was **pitch.** She needed to make a low sound for the roots and a high sound for the sky. Let's show her what to do.

"The roots are low, the roots are low," students said in a low pitch.

"That is the sound that you must know."

"The sky is high, the sky is high," students said in a high pitch.

"That is the sound that you must cry."

"Well, that's better!" croaked the frog, and he creaked open the door to let her in.

The music was beautiful. There were low-pitched cellos and bassoons and high-pitched violins and harps. All the fairies were dancing in beautiful, colorful, sparkling clothes.

But the door was too small; the little girl couldn't fit through. She was about to be very upset again, when the music stopped and all the fairies turned and looked at her.

"You want to join us? Well, if you can't come to us, we'll come to you!" So the fairy dancers and musicians came through the wooden door.

They danced away the afternoon, and the roots sang to them in a low pitch and the sky in its high pitch. When the little girl was called home for dinner, she said good-bye to her friends.

"Mama!" she exclaimed as she ran into the house. "I've had the most wonderful day! And I've learned about pitch!"

SOME IDEAS FOR LEARNING ABOUT PITCH

◎ Borrow some musical instruments from the music teacher or have students bring instruments from home. Make sure students know to treat each instrument with proper care. Students carefully observe ways each instrument makes high tones and low tones.

◎ Students make some inferences about pitch and test them. Some principles they may discover are that thicker strings make lower tones than thinner strings. Longer columns of air make lower tones than short columns. Larger drums make deeper sounds than smaller ones.

◎ Play two pieces of music for students, one piece primarily in a high range, another primarily in a low range. Invite students to draw or color an abstract picture elicited by each piece of music. Students compare their feelings, the colors used, and the general appearance of the pictures as they relate to the differences in pitch. What common elements exist in different students' pictures elicited by the same piece of music? These pictures, along with students' comments about the effect of the music on their art, might form the basis of an interesting bulletin board.

SOME WAYS TO USE THE STORY

◎ Students write and illustrate children's books that tell the story in their own words.

◎ Perhaps with the help of the music teacher, students identify pictures of or the actual musical instruments that could play the low and high pitches in the story.

◎ Students act out the story as they hear it. They hold their hands parallel to the floor, raise their hands when they hear high-pitched tones, and lower their hands when they hear low-pitched tones.

◎ Students recount the story in their own words. How they tell the story gives an authentic assessment of their understanding of the concept of pitch.

WEB ADDRESSES

http://www.fit.qut.edu.au/Student/ITB235/Structure/sound/sexhibt3.htm

This very long e-mail address will take you to an interesting site to learn about pitch. The site shows moving graphs that represent "squashed together" waves caused by fast vibrations that make high pitch and further apart waves from slow vibrations making low pitch. Since the height of the waves are the same, both graphs depict the same loudness.

http://www.sasked.gov.sk.ca/docs/physics/u5c22phy.html

This site provides background information about pitch for the teacher. The information includes the normal range of human hearing, infrasonic sound (below human hearing), and ultrasonic sound (above human hearing.) It also describes the unique properties of tuning forks.

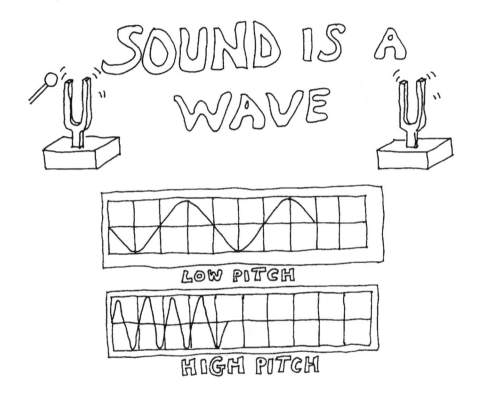

19

SYMMETRY

WITH BILATERAL SYMMETRY
BOTH SIDES LOOK THE SAME TO ME.
HOW DO I KNOW? MY EYES CAN TELL ME SO!

WHEN I LOOK AT GRANDMA'S SPECTACLES,
I CAN SEE THEY ARE SYMMETRICAL.
HOW DO I KNOW? MY EYES CAN TELL ME SO!

NOW RADIAL SYMMETRY
GOES ROUND AND ROUND AND ROUND YOU SEE.
HOW DO I KNOW? MY EYES CAN TELL ME SO!

AND RADIAL SYMMETRY
HAS MORE THAN ONE LINE OF SYMMETRY.
HOW DO I KNOW? MY EYES CAN TELL ME SO!

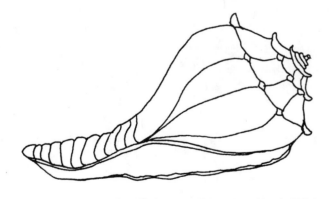

Symmetry

*Words and Music by
Kathleen Carroll*

1. With bi - lat - er - al sym-me - try
2. Now ra - di - al sym-me - try goes

both sides look the same to me.
round and round and round you see.

How do I know? My eyes can tell me so!

When I look at Grand - ma's spec - ta - cles, I can
And ra - di - al sym - me - try has

see than they are sym - me - tri - cal.
more than one line of sym - me - try.

How do I know? My eyes can tell me so!

eyes can tell me so!

21

Some Ideas for Learning about Symmetry

❁ One way to help students discover and understand concepts for themselves is through a concept attainment lesson. Show students two objects or pictures of objects. Place in the "yes" column the object that represents the concept you want students to discover. Place in the "no" column an object that does not represent the concept. Students naturally hypothesize about what makes one object "yes" and the other "no." Show additional pictures or objects one by one, and ask students to guess whether each is a "yes" or a "no." Each time a student makes a guess, ask for reasons. Accept any answer that is logical. Unless students are very young, start with objects After discussion about each object, place it in the proper column, then ask students if they want to revise their hypotheses. Eventually, objects in the "yes" column will narrow the hypotheses, leading students to the concept you originally chose. In the example on page 23, the concept is symmetry.

❁ Students go on a symmetry hunt. Using the definition in the song, students list bilateral- and radial-symmetrical objects they find in the classroom or at home.

❁ Students make a bulletin board for the classroom by cutting out magazine pictures that illustrate bilateral or radial symmetry.

❁ Students make shapes that show symmetry by putting a drop of ink or paint on a piece of paper, then carefully folding the paper in half. The result will be a beautiful, symmetrical design. Students have fun saying what the design looks like to them.

A Way to Use the Song

❁ Students tape down large pieces of paper on their desks, the blackboard, or the wall. Each student has a crayon, a marker, or a piece of chalk in each hand. As the music plays, students doodle with their hand motions mirroring each other. This exercise may do more than reinforce the concept of symmetry. According to many researchers, this exercise also helps students increase problem-solving skills.

Web Address

http://www-ed.fnal.gov/qtoq/tri_sq.html.

Find a problem for students to solve at this site. Students imagine triangles flipping over or spinning to the right, then decide whether or not the new designs still have symmetry.

YES	NO	HYPOTHESIS

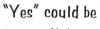

"Yes" could be
- nonliving
- humanmade
- symmetrical

"Yes" could be
- humanmade
- symmetrical

Surprise! Now "Yes" is living and "No" is nonliving and humanmade. But all the "Yeses" are symmetrical.

THE LEARNER DISCOVERS THE CONCEPT OF SYMMETRY.

WEATHER INSTRUMENTS RAP

WHETHER IT'S COLD, WHETHER IT'S WARM,
A SUNNY DAY OR IN A STORM,
THE WEATHER TO MEASURE
IS ALWAYS A PLEASURE!

THERMOMETERS YOU KNOW, I'M SURE,
SHOW DEGREES OF TEMPERATURE.
HYGROMETER'S THE ONE TO SEE
FOR PERCENTAGE OF HUMIDITY.

THE ANEMOMETER LETS YOU KNOW
HOW FAST THE WIND CAN BLOW.
THE WIND VANE, THOUGH, HELPS YOU IN KNOWING
THE DIRECTION THAT THE WIND IS BLOWING.

RAIN OR SNOW OR VERY FAIR —
WHAT'S THE PRESSURE OF THE AIR?
THAT IS WHY THE BAROMETER'S THERE,
TO FIND THE PRESSURE OF THE AIR.

WHETHER IT'S COLD, WHETHER IT'S WARM,
A SUNNY DAY OR IN A STORM,
THE WEATHER TO MEASURE
IS ALWAYS A PLEASURE!

PRECIPITATION

REFRAIN:

OH, THERE'RE FASCINATING FORMS OF PRECIPITATION.
YOU CAN HEAR IT ON THE NEWS OF YOUR TV STATION.
THERE ARE FASCINATING FORMS OF PRECIPITATION.
THE WET STUFF FALLS ALL AROUND OUR NATION.

WARM, MOIST AIR RISES AND FALLS BACK DOWN AS RAIN.
IF IT'S HAIL, IT FREEZES AND FALLS AND RISES
AGAIN AND AGAIN AND AGAIN.

[REFRAIN]

SNOW FORMS WHEN THE VAPOR FREEZES,
MAKES CRYSTALS NICE TO VIEW.
SLEET COMES WHEN THE RAIN JUST FREEZES
AND FALLS BACK DOWN ON YOU.

[REFRAIN]

Precipitation

Words and Music by
Kathleen Carroll

Oh there're fas - ci - na - ting forms of pre - ci - pi -

ta - tion._____ You can hear it on the news of your

T. V. sta - tion. There are fas - ci - na - ting forms of pre - ci - pi -

ta - tion.___ The wet stuff falls all a - round our na - tion.

1.Warm, moist the air ri - ses and
2.Snow forms when the va - por freez - es, makes

falls back down as rain. If it's
cry - stals nice to view.

hail it freez - es and falls and ri - ses a -
Sleet comes when the rain just freez - es and

gain and a - gain and a - gain.
falls back down on you.

THE WATER CYCLE

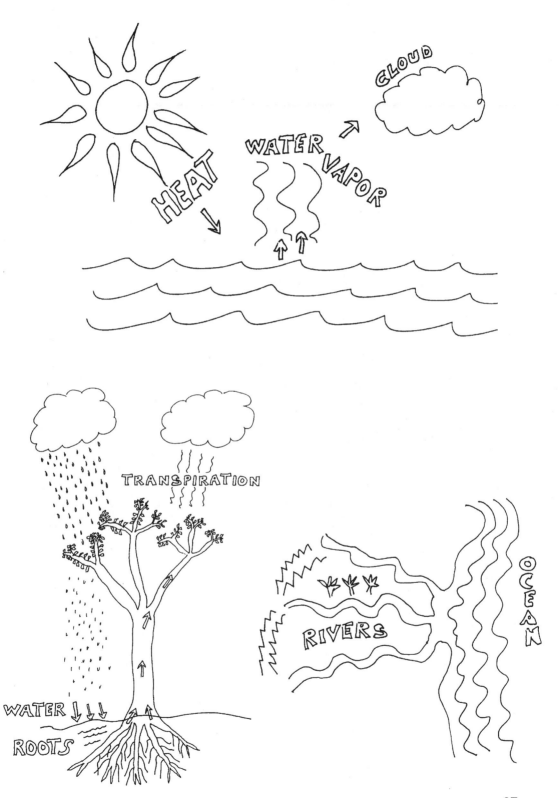

Sit down, relax, close your eyes. Imagine you are a drop of water in the vast blue ocean. There you are, on a wave, moving up and down, up and down. The sun shines warm upon you. After a while, you begin to get hot, for the sun is giving you energy. Suddenly, you pop into the air, evaporating. You are water vapor, invisible and free.

You float around for a long time. An updraft comes along and pushes you higher and higher up into the atmosphere, where it is cool. You move together with some other water vapor molecules. You condense back into water and become the rain. You fall gently to Earth. You soak into the ground and find yourself being sucked up by the roots of a tree. Up, up you flow, through the trunk, then out the leaves in transpiration. You are water vapor again. Now it is night; the air is cool and you condense and become the dew. Later, it rains and you flow into a stream, and the stream flows to the river, and the river to the vast blue ocean where you are a drop of water in a wave, moving up and down, up and down, and the sun shines warm upon you.

SOME IDEAS FOR LEARNING ABOUT WEATHER

Weather studies offer a wealth of hands-on activities for students to develop understanding of concepts. There is also a wealth of opportunities on the Internet. If you are not able to get on the web yet, your library will have a number of books with instructions for making a weather station. Many schools have available commercial weather instruments. The local newspaper should have weather maps that students can use to learn weather symbols.

- Setting up a weather station either with handmade or commercial instruments is an ideal way to study weather. When students collect and analyze data over time, they enhance their skills in scientific inquiry.

- Over your school's public address system, students present a weather forecast each day they are learning about weather. Learning is often enriched when students experience real-world applications of their studies.

SOME WAYS TO USE THE RAP, THE SONG, AND VISUALIZATION

- Like many of the songs in *Sing a Song of Science,* the "Weather Instruments Rap" helps students become familiar with vocabulary pertaining to the study of weather. Another way to reinforce memory of words and their definitions is to study the origins of the words. Ask students what the words *thermometer, hygrometer, anemometer,* and *barometer* have in common. (Each word contains the suffix *-meter.*) The suffix comes from the Greek and means "to measure." The prefix *anem-* also comes from the Greek and means "wind." Each root word describes exactly what the instrument measures.

- Students look at a weather map in your local newspaper and match the weather symbols to the types of precipitation found in "Precipitation." Students find out where the various types of precipitation are taking place in the world on a given day.

- Use visualizations such as "The Water Cycle" (page 27) as the basis for creative writing. Even students who are usually reluctant writers may enjoy such exercises.

WEB ADDRESSES

http://sln.fi.edu/weather/index.html

This is on Franklin Institute's web site. It gives step-by-step instructions for making weather instruments. The site also provides instructions on reading radar images and excellent Webweather sites. These sites include US and world maps. Click any place on the maps and get an immediate update on the weather in that area.

http://cirrus.sprl.umich.edu/wxnet

This is the address for WeatherNet. Enter a city, state, country, or zip code for a current weather forecast. WeatherNet has links to many interesting weather sites.

http://onesky.engin.umich.edu/

This is the site for "One Sky, Many Voices," a project designed to help middle school students all over North America and the world to collaboratively study weather events.

TROPICAL RAIN FOREST RAP

CANOPY

UNDERSTORY

FLOOR

REFRAIN:

THE TROPICAL RAIN FOREST IS A REAL SPECIAL PLACE
AND IT'S DISAPPEARING AT A VERY FAST PACE.
WHEN YOU FIND OUT ABOUT IT, I KNOW JUST WHAT YOU'LL DO.
YOU'LL WANT TO HELP TO SAVE IT, IT'S IMPORTANT TO YOU.

A WIDE GREEN BELT AROUND THE WORLD; FOR MILLIONS OF YEARS IT'S HAD
HALF EARTH'S PLANTS AND ANIMAL KINDS. TO LOSE IT WOULD BE SAD.

PLANTS LIKE YOU'LL SEE NOWHERE ELSE — INSECTS, FROGS, AND BIRDS AND
SNAKES;
MONKEYS SWINGING THROUGH THE TREES, LOTS OF COLORS, SIZES, SHAPES.

THE FLOOR HAS DARK AND OPEN SPACES. THE CANOPY IS THICK AND HIGH.
THE UNDERSTORY IN BETWEEN HAS THREE-TOED SLOTHS AND SNAKES THAT FLY.

THE RICHEST LIVING PLACE ON EARTH HAS SOMETHING VERY STRANGE.
IT'S SOIL IS VERY, VERY POOR. IT CAN'T SURVIVE A CHANGE.

THE FOREST IS A LIVING WEB, WHICH MEANS ONE PART NEEDS THE OTHER.
TAKE AWAY SOME FOREST HERE, YOU MAY FIND YOU KILL ANOTHER.

EARTH'S CLIMATE MAY GET HOTTER IF WE CUT THE FOREST AND
THE RAIN MAY STOP FROM FALLING, MAKING DESERTS OF OUR LAND.

PLANT MEDICINES TO CURE US MAY BE LOST ALONG THE WAY.
AND THE FOREST'S NATIVE PEOPLE WILL HAVE NO PLACE TO STAY.

[REFRAIN]

IF THE TROPICAL RAIN FOREST'S SUCH A VERY SPECIAL TREASURE, WHY WOULD WE DESTROY IT?
SOMETIMES NEED AND SOMETIMES PLEASURE.
IN SOME COUNTRIES MANY PEOPLE REALLY NEED A PLACE TO FARM.
THEY HAVE NO REAL INTENTION THERE TO DO THE FOREST HARM.

SO THE PLACE THEY CLEAR TO PLANT ON IN A YEAR OR MAYBE TWO
ERODES INTO A DESERT. THERE IS NOTHING THEY CAN DO. AND THEN THEY CUT SOME MORE.

AND PEOPLE CUT THE LUMBER FOR THEIR HOMES AND FOR FIREWOOD.
AND FOREIGN COUNTRIES TAKE IT CAUSE IT'S HARD AND IT LOOKS GOOD. AND THEY CUT SOME MORE.

THE CATTLE RANCHERS CUT IT DOWN TO MAKE HAMBURGERS CHEAP.
THAT'S WHEN THEY PLANT SOME GRASSES FOR THE CATTLE TO EAT. AND THEN THEY CUT SOME MORE.

THE POOR ENDANGERED ANIMALS ARE SHIPPED AWAY AND SOLD.
TO PET STORES AND COLLECTORS. THEY TAKE THE YOUNG AND KILL THE OLD.
AND THEN THEY TAKE SOME MORE.

AND WHAT CAN JUST ONE PERSON DO FOR SUCH A TRAGEDY?
EACH OF US CAN COME ALONG AND DO SOME THINGS, LIKE ME.

[REFRAIN]

INDIVIDUAL STUDENTS

MY NAME IS KEVIN, MY AGE IS SEVEN, AND HERE'S THE WAY I GO:
I LEARN AS MUCH AS I CAN ABOUT THE WHOLE PROBLEM,
THEN I TELL THE NEWS TO EVERYONE I KNOW.

MY NAME IS BEN, MY AGE IS TEN, AND I'LL DO KEVIN ONE BETTER:
I LEARN WHAT'S NEW THAT OUR GOVERNMENT CAN DO,
AND THEN I WRITE MY CONGRESSMAN A LETTER.

MY NAME IS HONEY, I GIVE MY MONEY TO HELP PEOPLE, ANIMALS, AND PLANTS.
I JOIN WITH GROUPS THAT HAVE THE SCOOP AND I SAY
"WE CAN" TO THOSE WHO SAY "WE CAN'T."

MY NAME IS MICHAEL, AND I RECYCLE PAPER, PLASTIC, BOTTLES, SODA CANS.
AND IT'S EASY TO SEE, IF YOU ALL DO LIKE ME,
WE'LL HELP TO SAVE THE FUTURE OF OUR LAND.

MY NAME IS GRANT, AND I SAVE PLANTS AND ANIMALS RIGHT HERE IN MY
BACKYARD.
I GROW THE RIGHT SEEDS AND THE BIRDS I FEED,
THEY'RE HAPPY AND IT ISN'T VERY HARD.

MY NAME IS JEANNETTE, I ONLY GET A PET THAT WAS BORN IN THE U. S. OF A.
WE CAN SAVE THE REST FOR THE RAIN FOREST
SO THEIR KIND WILL GET TO LIVE ANOTHER DAY.

[GROUP]

WE GO TO A SCHOOL THAT IS FUN AND REALLY COOL;
WE MAKE POSTERS, PLAYS, AND SONGS AND ESSAYS, TOO.
WE MAKE THIS SHOW TO LET OTHERS KNOW
THAT THERE IS SOMETHING ALL OF US CAN DO.

REFRAIN:

THE TROPICAL RAIN FOREST IS A REAL SPECIAL PLACE
AND IT'S DISAPPEARING AT A VERY FAST PACE.
NOW YOU KNOW MORE ABOUT IT, I KNOW JUST WHAT YOU'LL DO.
YOU'LL WANT TO HELP TO SAVE IT, YOU'VE GOT TO HELP SAVE IT.
WON'T YOU PLEASE HELP TO SAVE IT? IT'S IMPORTANT TO YOU.

The Tropical Rain Forest

Words and Music by
Kathleen Carroll

The tro-pi-cal rain for-est is a real spe-cial place and it's
dis - ap-pear - ing at a ver - y fast pace. (1..3.)When you

(4.)Now you
find out a-bout it, I know just what you'll do. You'll

know more...
want to help to save it, it's im - por- tant to you.

want to help to save it, you've got to help to save it. *Won't you please help to save it?*

(spoken)

It's im- por- tant to you.

IDEAS FOR LEARNING ABOUT
THE TROPICAL RAIN FOREST

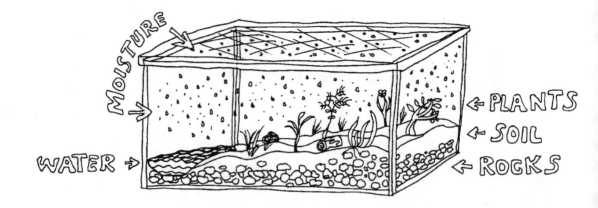

✾ Students use a glass jar or an old glass aquarium to make a terrarium as a model of the rain forest. They place rocks along the bottom for drainage. They add sand, then soil, making mountains and valleys. They make an interesting scene with plants and rocks to represent the canopy, the understory, and the floor, adding a worm or some insects to represent wildlife.

✾ Using murals and pictures drawn on butcher paper, crepe paper, real and artificial plants, and pictures of animals and toy animals, students help you turn the classroom into a tropical rain forest. Layers of the forests go on the appropriate places on the walls and ceiling, with appropriate animals at each level. Let students take off with their imaginations. Music such as "Heart of the Forest" or "Rain Forest Dreams" add another dimension. Invite other classes to visit. Groups of your students could present information on various aspects of the tropical rain forest at centers in the tropical rain forest room.

✾ World Wildlife Fund has a video of a "Rain Forest Rap" with some beautiful footage of the tropical rain forest, which lends itself to many classroom activities. To order, phone WWF's fulfillment office at (410) 516-6951.

✾ Students take part in a simulation, such as one my students did of a meeting about the future of a particular piece of land in the tropical rain forest. Students were representatives from different interest groups, including ranchers, a pharmaceutical company, indigenous people, and animals. They had a good time researching their characters' points of view and dressing up for their parts.

SOME WAYS TO USE THE RAP

❋ Students make a Mind Map or a class mural that depicts the information in "Tropical Rain Forest Rap."

❋ Using the student examples in the rap, students brainstorm and write raps about ways they might contribute to the preservation of the tropical rain forest. They make action plans for the most appealing and possible choices.

WEB ADDRESSES

http://nwf.org/nwf/action/howtos/index.html

This is the National Wildlife Foundation's web site with "How to's for Activists," which includes raising money, dealing with the media, writing to your lawmaker, and more. There is a children's rain forest preserve in Costa Rica.

http://www.wwf.org/forests/

Another part of the web site of the World Wildlife Fund, this site includes a map of the world. Click on any place near the equator and a map of the tropical rain forest of that country becomes visible.

http://www.kidlink.org/KIDPROJ/Sumatra/

Take a virtual trip to the topical rain forest in Sumatra and learn about the endangered orangutans there. This trip is courtesy of an American School in Saudi Arabia. A class in this school went to the rain forests in Sumatra and sent mail to KIDLINK.

http://www.kidlink.org/

This is the web site for KIDLINK. The goal of KIDLINK is to help young people from ten to fifteen years of age enter into global dialogue through e-mail and other telecommunication exchanges.

From Slave to Botanical Genius

GEORGE WASHINGTON CARVER

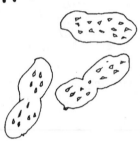

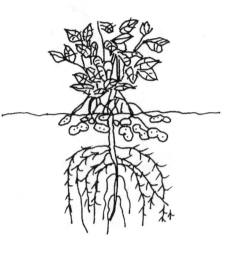

A long time ago in Missouri, a slave baby and his mother were stolen by out-laws. Their master, Moses Carver, offered the outlaws a race horse in return for them. The outlaws returned the baby, but not the mother.

Now this baby was so sickly that no one thought he would live. But he did. After the Civil War, when slavery was abolished, he still lived with the Carver family. He was called George Washington Carver.

Now little George was too small and weak to work in the fields, so he helped Mrs. Carver in the house. His favorite pastime was taking care of the plants. George knew just how much water and sun and just what kind of soil each plant needed. He also knew how to start plants from seeds. He knew about the little baby plant, the embryo, inside the seed. He knew how it eats the food in the seed as its roots grow down in the soil and its stem and leaves grow up to the sun. Neighbors from all around brought their sick plants to George to heal them. He had a green thumb.

George wanted very much to go to school, but in those days and in that place, black people weren't allowed to go to school. So George walked a long way to live in another town where they allowed black people to go to school. He found places where he could work in exchange for food and a night's sleep, and he studied every chance he got. Soon he knew as much as his teachers knew, so he decided to move on to another school. George did very well at his new school, so well that he got a schol-arship to college. When he arrived at the college, the president was very surprised.

"I had no idea that your skin was black," he said. "Of course, we can't accept you here."

George was very sad. He gave up. But after a few years some kind people helped him get admitted to another college, Iowa State University.

He could have studied art. He was a fine artist. He could have studied music. George was an excellent pianist. But he returned instead to his greatest love—botany, the study of plants.

George started a laundry business. He washed his fellow students' shirts to pay his way through school.

George got his BS and Ph.D. degrees and was making a very good life for himself when, one day, he received a letter from Booker T. Washington at Tuskegee Institute, a college for black people in Alabama. Washington wanted George to come to Tuskegee to teach botany. George thought and thought. Should he leave his fine new life? But Washington offered him a chance to help poor students such as he had been. Finally, he decided. George went to Tuskegee and stayed there the rest of his life.

When he arrived, he found there were no labs, no equipment—nothing to work with. So he sent his students on scavenger hunts for old jars and cans and tables.

The South was very poor at that time. They had lost the war, and their soil was worn out from planting too much cotton and tobacco. George Washington Carver and his students took a wagon from farm to farm to show farmers how to rotate crops to improve the soil. They taught farmers to plant peanuts one year to put nitrogen in the soil, then plant cotton or tobacco the next year. Many farmers did what Carver told them to, but soon they had a problem and they blamed it on Carver. "What are we supposed to do with these dumb peanuts?" they shouted angrily. "They aren't good for anything but eating at the circus or feeding to the hogs!"

Carver walked slowly back to his laboratory. He shut the door and didn't come out for a week. The others at Tuskegee were concerned. What's happened to him? Has he lost his mind?

Finally, Carver opened the door. There, to everyone's amazement, were dozens of inventions—new uses for the peanut. He made salad oil, butter, cheese, shaving cream, plastics out of peanuts. Before long, he had invented more than three hundred uses for the peanut. And peanuts became a more valuable crop than tobacco. He also found many uses for the sweet potato and soy beans.

George Washington Carver, a man who was born a slave, may have done more than anyone else to save the South. When he died, people all over the world were sad at the loss of this brilliant, brave, and humble man.

THE LIFE CYCLE
OF A PLANT

In this next story, students pretend to be a baby plant inside a seed. They can either act it out or close their eyes and imagine it happening.

Squat down into a little ball on the floor and pretend to be a baby plant, an embryo inside a seed. You have been asleep for a long time. Your seed coat has been protecting you. Now the rain comes and you wake up. You are hungry. As you eat the food inside the seed, you begin to grow. Your roots push through the seed coat and into the ground. Your stem and leaves pop through, too. Slowly stand up as you grow and grow and grow. Your leaves are turning the sun's energy into food for you to grow.

Soon, something beautiful happens. You make a flower. It could be red or yellow, blue or even green. Then the bees and butterflies come for your nectar. They bring pollen to you.

Then you are sad. Your beautiful flower petals are falling. But wait. Something wonderful is happening! In place of the flower, a fruit is growing. Now its seeds are dropping all around you. Your babies are starting to grow!

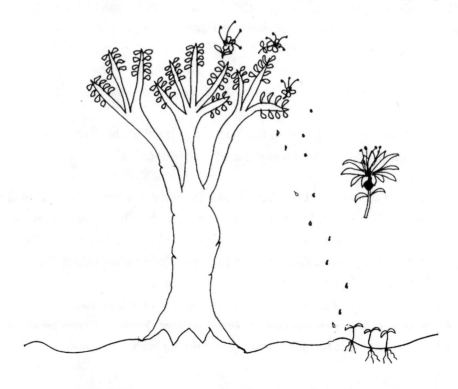

SOME IDEAS FOR LEARNING ABOUT PLANTS

☑ Students follow this process to make peanut butter the natural way.

1. Students wash their hands with soap and water. Give each group of four students peanuts in shells, a plastic bag with a zipper lock, a kindergarten-type wooden block, a paper cup with one tablespoon vegetable oil, napkins, a plastic spoon, and some crackers.

2. Students each take a peanut and observe it. Tell them that a peanut is a fruit, sometimes with multiple seeds inside. Review the way a seed grows.

3. Students crack the shells and find the three parts of one of the seeds. Students find these parts in soaked lima beans or other seeds, as well.

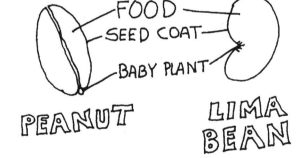

4. Students crack and skin several more peanuts and place the seeds in the plastic bag. Each student in the group takes a turn smashing the peanuts in the plastic bag with the wooden block. This experience is very noisy and satisfying for students. Allow students to continue hammering until the peanuts are chunky or smooth, whichever they prefer, or until you can't stand the noise anymore.

5. Students place the ground-up peanuts in the cup with oil and comment on the physical changes of matter.
6. Students mix the oil and nuts and spread on the crackers.
7. Students enjoy their snacks and thank George Washington Carver for them.

A Way to Use the Story and Songs

Students learn about other people from a variety of ethnic backgrounds who contributed to science.

Web Addresses

http://www.fi.edu/tfi/units/life/

At this site, the Franklin Institute Science Museum provides an online curriculum for living things.

http://nyelabs.kcts.org/nyeverse/episode/e43.html

The Science Guy has activities relating to plants, too. This site has an experiment students can do that shows that green plants make food and oxygen.

HOW ANIMALS MOVE

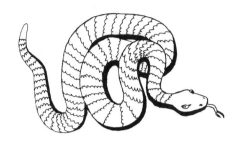

HOP, HOP, HOP, GOES THE BUNNY AND FROG,
WHILE THE HORSE AND DOG WALK BY.
SLITHER GOES THE SNAKE. NOW DON'T MAKE A MISTAKE.
SEE THE BIRDS FLY HIGH IN THE SKY.

CRAWL, CRAWL, CRAWL GOES THE ANT UPON THE WALL,
WHILE THE FISH AND DUCK SWIM BY.
THE MONKEY'S VERY PLEAS'D TO BE SWINGING THROUGH THE TREES.
BUTTERFLIES FLY HIGH IN THE SKY.
BUTTERFLIES FLY HIGH IN THE SKY.

41

How Animals Move

Words and Music by
Kathleen Carroll

SOME IDEAS FOR LEARNING ABOUT ANIMAL MOVEMENT

- Take your class on a walk through the neighborhood or a nearby park; students have tally sheets to record the types of animal locomotion they observe. They look for flying animals, such as birds and insects; walking animals, such as dogs and cats; climbing animals, such as squirrels and chipmunks; and, perhaps by digging a little and looking closely, crawling animals, such as snails and worms.

- Buy some inexpensive feeder fish (fish that are raised specifically to feed larger pets) from your local pet store. Place individual fish in large glasses or jars with dechlorinated water. Students look carefully at how the fish move, coming to consensus about which fins help the fish move forward, to the side, and so on.

- Set up stations with live animals, pictures, and reference material to offer students an effective way to observe animals. Animals could include invertebrates, such as hermit crabs and mealworms; fish; amphibians, such as frogs and newts; reptiles, such as snakes and lizards; birds, such as parakeets and canaries; and mammals, such as gerbils and hamsters. I have had success borrowing animals from other classrooms and from the pet store. Students are usually happy to bring in pets from home, too. Students make their own animal books based on the stations.

SOME WAYS TO USE THE SONG

- Form cooperative learning teams by giving each student a picture or name of an animal mentioned in the song. Make four or five copies of the same animal. Students move around the class in the manner that their animals would, looking for the rest of their "family."

- Students play animal charades, acting out the movement of a particular animal while others guess the animal's identity. The winner takes on the behavior of a new animal.

WEB ADDRESSES

http://nyelabs.kcts.org/nyeverse/episode/e60.html

This is Bill Nye, the Science Guy's, site for weird facts about animal movements and an activity through which students can learn about animal locomotion by studying animal tracks.

http://www.ceismc.gatech.edu/BusyT/

Busy teachers' web site provides a wealth of classroom activities on animal movement and many other subjects.

http://www.zooregon.org/

Take a virtual trip to the zoo with this site sponsored by the Metro Washington Park Zoo in Portland, Oregon. Students find out about animals and get information for school reports.

http://www.petsource.com/ASKDR.HTM

Ask Dr. Jim is a site where a veterinarian answers questions about pets' health and nutrition.

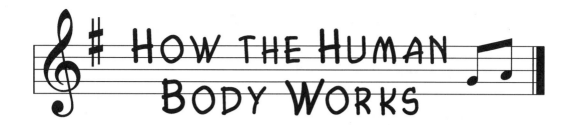

HOW THE HUMAN BODY WORKS

ENERGY COMES FROM THE CELL
TO HELP YOU MOVE AND GROW SO WELL.
WHEN FOOD COMBINES WITH OXYGEN,
HERE'S HOW IT GOES FROM START TO END.

RESPIRATION IS BREATHING IN AND OUT.
BUT THERE'S MUCH MORE TO THIS STORY.
THAT'S WHAT THIS SONG'S ABOUT.
DOWN GOES THE DIAPHRAGM
AND PULLS THE OXYGEN IN.
FROM NOSE, WINDPIPE AND BRONCHIAL TUBES
THE JOURNEY MUST BEGIN.
FROM LUNGS TO HEART TO BLOOD STREAM,
AND RIGHT INTO THE CELL.
THE ENERGY CAN NOW BE MADE.
YOUR BODY'S DOING SWELL.

DIGESTION IS BREAKING DOWN YOUR FOOD.
BUT THERE'S MUCH MORE TO THIS STORY.
SO GET IN A LISTENING MOOD.
YOUR TEETH WILL CHEW IT UP,
SALIVA GETS THE STARCH.
FROM ESOPHAGUS TO STOMACH
THAT LUMP OF FOOD MUST MARCH.
THE STOMACH CHURNS IT ROUND
AND SENDS ITS ACIDS IN.
DIGESTION GETS ALL FINISHED IN
THE SMALL INTESTINE.

CIRCULATION MAKES BLOOD GO ROUND AND ROUND.
BUT THERE'S MUCH MORE TO THIS STORY.
SO STOP AND STICK AROUND.
THE HEART PUMPS THE BLOOD SO WELL
INSIDE OF YOU AND ME.
WITH FOOD AND OXYGEN WE NEED
TO MAKE SOME ENERGY.
THEN BLOOD CLEARS THE BODY OF
THE WASTE AND CO_2.
AND THAT'S THE WAY THE STORY GOES
INSIDE OF ME AND YOU.

ENERGY COMES FROM THE CELL
TO HELP YOU GROW AND RUN AND SPELL.
WHEN FOOD COMBINES WITH OXYGEN
THAT'S HOW IT WENT FROM START TO END.

How the Human Body Works Song

Words and Music by
Kathleen Carroll

lungs to heart to blood stream, and right in - to the cell. The
sto - mach churns it round and sends its a - cids in. Di -
blood clears the bo - dy of the waste and C - O - 2. And

D.C. al Fine

en - er - gy can now be made. Your bo - dy's do - ing swell.
ges - tion gets all fin - ish'd in the small in - tes - tine.
that's the way the sto - ry goes in - side of me and you.

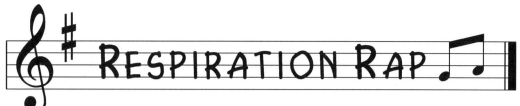

RESPIRATION RAP

BY MARC GIBSON, 6TH GRADE

WELL, YOU BREATHE IT OUT
AND YOU BREATHE IT IN
AND THE RESPIRATORY SYSTEM
IS ABOUT TO BEGIN.
TO THE LUNGS, TO THE HEART,
AND TO THE CELL —
THE OXYGEN KEEPS YOUR BODY WELL.
UP, UP, AND OUT THE NOSE —
THAT'S WHERE THE CARBON DIOXIDE GOES.

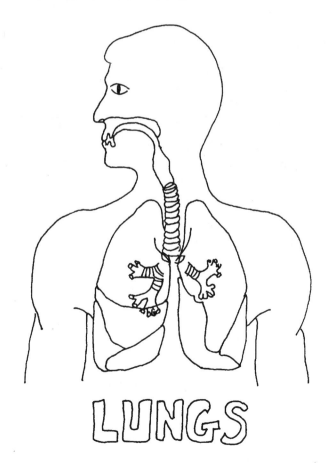

LUNGS

SOME IDEAS FOR LEARNING ABOUT HUMAN BODY SYSTEMS

❉ Students take their pulses by placing their index and middle fingers on their necks about an inch below their jaws, midway between the ear and chin. By counting the pulse for ten seconds and multiplying by six, they will have their pulse rates per minute. Students do jumping jacks for sixty seconds, then take their pulses again. Students put on backpacks with books in them and repeat the experiment. The pulse should be fastest the third time because their bodies are working harder to get the oxygen and energy needed to exercise. Students may infer that having excess weight can be hard on your heart.

❉ Cut off the bottom of a plastic soda bottle. Stick a small balloon upside down in the mouth of the bottle, and pull the mouth of the balloon over the bottle's lip. Cut a larger balloon or punch ball so that you can spread it over the bottom of the bottle. Tape the edges of the large balloon around the bottle. When you pull down on the large balloon, the bottle gets bigger making more room for air, so the small balloon fills with air. The lungs work on the same principle. When the diaphragm (compare to the big balloon) goes down, the chest cavity gets bigger and the lungs fill with air. See Bill Nye's web site for more ideas on this activity.

❉ Students trace outlines of one another's bodies on butcher paper. As they study each system, they draw and label the organs, cut them out, and place them on the outline.

SOME WAYS TO USE THE SONG AND THE RAP

❉ Students use "How the Human Body Works" and "Respiratory Rap" as models for writing their own songs and raps.

❉ Students write metaphors and similes to develop bridges between what they know and what they are learning. My sixth-grade students wrote similes for the systems of the human body described in the song and drew pictures to go along with the similes. "Scientific Similes" turned out to be a very interesting bulletin board.

WEB ADDRESSES

http://nyelabs.kcts.org/nyeverse/episode/e76.html

The activities based on the heart and lungs were adapted from activities provided at this site.

http://www.innerbody.com/indexbody.html

This site provides interactive anatomy graphics for each system of the human body. Touch various parts of the graphics and get the name of the organ depicted. The site also provides eighteen pages of anatomy lessons.

REFERENCES

Brewer, C., and D. Campbell. 1991. *Rhythms of Learning: Creative Tools for Developing Lifelong Skills.* Tucson, Ariz.: Zephyr Press.
> Presents many ways that rhythm and music can be used to enhance classroom learning and enjoyment.

Buzan, T. 1983. *Use Both Sides of Your Brain: New Techniques to Help You Read Efficiently, Study Effectively, Solve Problems, Remember More, Think Creatively.* rev. ed. New York: Dutton.
> Includes a detailed description of how, when, and why to mind map.

Checkley, K. 1997. "The First Seven . . . and the Eighth." *Educational Leadership* 55: 8–13.
> Uses Gardner's words to describe the naturalist intelligence in an issue dedicated to teaching for multiple intelligences.

Clark, Barbara. 1986. *Optimizing Learning: The Interactice Education Model in the Classroom.* Columbus, Ohio: Merrill.
> Shows ways to integrate cognitive, physical, sensory, intuitive, and affective into all areas of education.

Diamond, M. 1985. "Cortical Plasticity Induced by Experience and Sex Hormones." Paper presented at the California Neuropsychological Services Conference, San Raphael, California.

Dryden, G., and J. Vos. 1994. *The Learning Revolution: A Life-Long Learning Program for the World's Finest Computer—Your Amazing Brain!* Rolling Hills Estates, Calif.: Jalmar Press.
> Summarizes research in a wide range of disciplines and synthesizes it in a new theory for the learning society.

Gardner, H. 1983. *Frames of Mind.* New York: Basic.
> Describes the research that led to Gardner's theory of the multiple intelligences.

Hannaford, C. 1995. *Smart Moves: Why Learning Is Not All in Your Head.* Arlington, Va.: Great Ocean.
> Presents scientific research on the effects of movement, the arts, and nutrition on learning; emphasizes specific ways to apply the research to enhance learning.

Harris, J. 1998. *Design Tools for the Internet-Supported Classroom.* Alexandria, Va.: ASCD.
> Provides structure, processes, and resources for teachers and students to design successful Internet projects.

Jensen, E. P. 1995. *Brain-Based Learning and Teaching.* Del Mar, Calif.: Turning Point.
> Describes research for boosting motivation, attention, and understanding; includes use of music to enhance learning.

Lozanov, G. 1981. *Suggestology and Outlines of Suggestopedia.* New York: Gordon and Breach.

Margulies, N., and R. Sylwester. 1998b. *Emotion and Attention: How Our Brain Determines What's Important.* Discover Your Brain series. Tucson, Ariz.: Zephyr Press.
> Provides multimodal (audiotape, booklet, poster) approaches to understanding one part of the learning system.

———. 1998b. *Memory: Acquiring, Editing, Recalling, Forgetting.* Discover Your Brain series. Tucson, Ariz.: Zephyr Press.
> Provides multimodal (audiotape, booklet, poster) approaches to understanding one part of the learning system.

Sylwester, R. 1995. *A Celebration of Neurons: An Educator's Guide to the Human Brain.* Alexandria, Va.: ASCD.
> Applies insights from brain theory and research to the improvement of schools.

Wenger, W., and R. Poe. 1996. *The Einstein Factor: A Proven Method for Increasing Your Intelligence.* Rocklin, Calif.: Prima.
> Offers innovative tools to reach greater levels of sharpness, insight, and overall intelligence.

Motivate your students to use all 8 intelligences including the <u>NATURALIST INTELLIGENCE</u>

DISCOVERING THE NATURALIST INTELLIGENCE
Science in the School Yard
by Jenna Glock, Susan Wertz, and Maggie Meyer
foreword by Thomas R. Hoerr, Ph.D.
Grades 1–6

It's what you've been waiting for! Apply this fresh approach to your curriculum and watch students come alive! By popular demand, here is the tool you need to help you—

- Define what the naturalist intelligence is and can achieve
- Identify naturalist traits in your students with an observational checklist
- Meet national science standards while using MI techniques in every lesson
- Strengthen your students' use of the naturalist intelligence with more than 30 outdoor lessons

All activities can be completed after a focused excursion into the average school yard or playground.
1095-W . . . $29

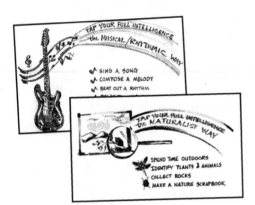

TAP YOUR MULTIPLE INTELLIGENCES
Posters for the Classroom
text by David Lazear
illustrations by Nancy Margulies
Grades 3–12

This handy set of 8 colorful posters will remind your students to use all their intelligences. Each poster reinforces a specific intelligence. Includes the naturalist!

8 full-color, 11" x 17" posters.
1811-W . . . $27

Order Form
Call, Write, or FAX for your FREE Catalog!

Qty.	Item #	Title	Unit Price	Total
	1095-W	Discovering the Naturalist Intelligence	$29	
	1811-W	Tap Your Multiple Intelligences	$27	

Name _____

Address _____

City _____

State _____ Zip _____

Phone (_____) _____

E-mail _____

Subtotal	
Sales Tax (AZ residents, 5%)	
S & H (10% of Subtotal, min. $4.00)	
Total (U.S. Funds only)	

CANADA: add 22% for S & H and G.S.T.

Method of payment (check one):

❑ Check or Money Order ❑ Visa

❑ MasterCard ❑ Purchase Order Attached

Credit Card No. _____

Expires _____

Signature _____

Zephyr Press ®
REACHING THEIR HIGHEST POTENTIAL

To order write or call:
P.O. Box 66006-W
Tucson, AZ 85728-6006
1-800-232-2187
FAX 520-323-9402
http://www.zephyrpress.com